A Planning Guide for

Information Power

Building Partnerships for Learning

with
School Library
Media Program
Assessment Rubric
for the 21st Century

Prepared by the AMERICAN ASSOCIATION OF SCHOOL LIBRARIANS,
a division of the AMERICAN LIBRARY ASSOCIATION
Edited by Donald C. Adcock
AMERICAN ASSOCIATION OF SCHOOL LIBRARIANS
AMERICAN LIBRARY ASSOCIATION
Chicago 1999

Cover design by Angela Hanshaw, ALA Production Services. Interior text and composition by N&M Design and Type, Elmhurst, Illinois in Helvetica and Sabon.

Printed on 60-pound Finch Opaque, a pH-neutral stock, and bound in 10-pt C1S cover stock by Batson Printing.

The paper used in this publication meets the minimum requirements of American National Standards for Information Sciences—Permanence of Paper for Printed Library Materials, ANSI Z39.48-1992.

ISBN 0-8389-8073-2

Published by:
American Association of School Librarians
a division of the American Library Association
50 E. Huron St.
Chicago, Illinois 60611-2795
To order, call 800-545-2433, press 7

03   5 4 3 2

This document is designed to guide you through the planning process central to program development and implementation. Principles 5 and 6 in Chapter 6: "Program Administration" of *Information Power: Building Partnerships for Learning* provide planning goals for the library media specialist. Using this workbook, you will be able to focus your thinking (Leadership) on implementing a process that will maximize your personal resources and the support of the school community within a reasonable time frame (Planning) to achieve a plan of action to upgrade student achievement as well as to improve your school library media program for students and staff (Management).

Contents

Preface vii

Introduction ix

The Planning Process 1

Preparing for the Planning Process 2

Planning the First Committee Meeting 8

Developing Your Mission Statement 10

Developing Goals and Objectives 13

Collecting Needed Information 17

Developing Action Plans 20

Evaluating the Library Media Program 22

One Final Word 24

Action Plan Worksheet 26

School Library Media Program Assessment
Rubric for the 21st Century

Subcommittee members 30

Introduction 31

Scenarios 33

Assessment Rubric 34

Glossary of Terms 42

School Policies 44

Bibliography 45

Preface

Along with the publication of *Information Power: Guidelines for School Library Media Programs* in 1988, a guide was developed to assist library media specialists plan for the implementation of these new guidelines. The document proved to be very useful, leading the task force coordinating the implementation of the 1998 national guidelines, published in *Information Power: Building Partnerships for Learning*, to suggest the development of a similar document related to the 1998 guidelines.

Copies of the existing planning guide were examined and the planning sequence it utilized, as well as the introduction by Karen Whitney, was found to be as relevant today as when they were created in 1988. Some minor editorial changes to the text were necessary to reflect current thinking concerning information literacy standards for student learning and the role of library media specialists brought about by changes in society, education, and technology.

While there has been a shift in content from a primary focus on the roles of the media specialist, as presented in the 1988 guidelines, to a focus on student learning outcomes, as presented in the 1998 guidelines, the need for careful planning to implement the guidelines remains. As you develop your plan for implementing the new guidelines, utilize the planning process described in this manual to assist you. Time spent working through the sequential steps presented in this document, along with the rubric, will bring about desired improvements to the school library media program in your school or district. Systematic planning is time consuming, but necessary if you want to implement real change.

M. Ellen Jay
AASL President, 1999-2000

Introduction

A *Planning Guide* is designed to assist you in achieving the outstanding, comprehensive library media program outlined in *Information Power: Building Partnerships for Learning*. The program described in that book, published by the American Library Association and the Association for Educational Communications and Technology, is quite different from programs described in previous national standards or guidelines.

In *Information Power: Building Partnerships for Learning*, library media specialists are challenged to assume new responsibilities as they become a full partner on the school's instructional team. This new vision for the school library media program will not be achieved easily; however, careful planning and an honest commitment to involving your principal, teachers, and the community in the planning process will result in a program that is an integral part of the learning environment.

Before beginning the planning process it is necessary to examine the major emphases in *Information Power: Building Partnerships for Learning* to gain an overview of the differences between this document and previous guidelines. This overview will help you understand the significant shifts in thinking that are needed to reshape the library media program. Four key concepts presented in *Information Power: Building Partnerships for Learning* are significant in this reshaping:

1. **The need to create a library media program which provides a foundation for lifelong learning by combining effective learning and teaching strategies and activities with information access skills (taught through the existing curricula of the school) that will ensure that all students can interact effectively with information and construct meaningful knowledge.**

Educators in each school or district must use the information literacy standards for student learning to create and maintain a program that allows students to become skillful consumers and producers of information. The teaching of traditional library skills as a separate curriculum must cease. Educators must acknowledge that students are active and engaged users of information resources as the means to meeting their personal and instructional information needs; therefore, teaching library skills in isolation is inappropriate and ineffective. Library media specialists have a responsibility to articulate this position to their principal, teachers, and other individuals in their educational community and gain their support for this new approach.

2. **The recognition of the four roles of the library media specialist:**
   Information Specialist
   Teacher
   Instructional Partner
   Program Administrator

The mission of the library media program can only be accomplished through the performance of these four roles, sometimes separately, often in concert with each other. The ability to function effectively in these roles depends upon the ability to plan and manage the library media program.

3. The acknowledgment that the individual library media program cannot contain all the resources needed by students and staff; therefore, the program must provide access to resources beyond the school.

The library media collection must include points of access to information resources located outside the school. Providing convenient and timely access to the resources contained beyond the school's collection is a major responsibility of the library media program.

4. The emphasis on using a systematic planning process for developing the local library media program. This group process includes defining the mission, setting goals and objectives, assessing needs, implementing the program, and evaluating progress toward goals. The planning process is a continuous one that reshapes the library media program in light of changing needs.

The planning process will determine the goals and objectives of the program and strategies for reaching those goals, and the resources, both human and material, that are needed to implement the program. Means of evaluating progress toward attaining the goals will be identified. The planning process cannot be undertaken by library media specialists working alone. To integrate the library media program completely into the instructional program of the school, the principal, teachers and others must participate with the library media specialists in the planning process.

As you can see, *Information Power: Building Partnerships for Learning* establishes a new direction for library media programs. It also recognizes that each library media program will be different because each must be developed to anticipate and meet the unique needs of the local school. For this reason, a uniformly prescriptive approach to assessing the current program and to planning change is not practical. Each school must determine how it can best accomplish the mission of ensuring that all students and staff are effective users of information.

Library media specialists must provide the leadership to initiate the planning process in their schools. The planning sequence in this manual can assist you as you function as an agent of change to provide the process for improving the learning environment for all students. Only through this process can you ensure the library media program meets the needs of the school. Library media specialists alone can provide the leadership in their schools to accomplish the mission of *Information Power: Building Partnerships for Learning*.

Karen Whitney
AASL President, 1987-88
Statement Revised 1999

The Planning Process

You are the leader...

So here you are, a copy of *Information Power: Building Partnerships for Learning* in your hand, wondering, "Can I really use these guidelines to help students become proficient users of information today? Can I help them become information literate for the twenty-first century? Can a supportive team be created to initiate and implement the planning process? How can I accomplish my objectives?"

With all the daily demands from students and staff, it is easy to put off initiating a thorough planning process that systematically examines all aspects of the school's library media program. However, sound planning is the key to creating a quality library media program that meets and anticipates the needs of its users.

Systematic planning takes time, perseverance, and resources. It won't be easy, but a quality library media program is certainly worth the effort. Furthermore, you have experience, determination, and commitment. Don't underestimate these qualities. In addition, don't forget your library media center supporters, including members of your staff, parent and/or student groups with whom you have worked, members of the faculty and administration, and other members of the school community. These individuals will be invaluable in your planning efforts. It's time to begin!

Preparing for the Planning Process

Vision—where all planning begins...

What is your personal vision of the ideal library media center program? You may not think that you have a vision or philosophy, but you do. As you work each day in your library media center, you are, consciously or unconsciously, carrying out your vision or philosophy. Think about your vision and consider how it relates to the mission statement in chapter 1 of *Information Power: Building Partnerships for Learning.*

> The mission of the library media program is to ensure that students and staff are effective users of ideas and information. (p. 6)

This statement may present a different mission than you have considered in the past. No longer do library media programs merely support the curriculum and provide materials to meet students' instructional and personal information needs. These functions are still part of the library media program, but the program described in *Information Power: Building Partnerships for Learning* has moved beyond such a limited scope. School library media specialists must now accept a larger responsibility, one that focuses on helping students and staff effectively use information and ideas.

While the overarching mission of the school library media program is changing in its perspective, in many ways it builds on the traditional focus. We have always been concerned with providing information to students and teachers. The emphasis is shifting from merely locating information to using it effectively. Library media specialists are now concerned with a much broader and more comprehensive program, one that considers information use in its totality.

It is incumbent upon us to be concerned that:
- our students appreciate the value of information in meeting their personal and educational needs
- they develop positive attitudes toward the types of learning that will enable them to continue the learning process beyond their years of formal education
- they do become lifelong learners.

Most of all we must be concerned with how effectively our students use information. We must recognize that information is a means to an end. We must address the thought processes that enable students to:
- identify their information needs
- develop strategies for locating that information
- comprehend and evaluate the information they find
- synthesize that new information
- integrate that new information with background knowledge
- use the combination effectively to meet a current need.

Thus, the major difference between *Information Power: Building Partnerships for Learning* and former national standards or guidelines is the emphasis on the necessity for schools to define an "information curriculum" that can be developed throughout their existing curricula. The information curriculum cannot be isolated or separated from ongoing classroom curricula. Learning how to find and use information effectively is an integral part of every subject taught. Thus, developing an information curriculum must be a shared responsibility of the entire educational community.

As your school's library media specialist, you must provide the leadership for addressing this responsibility. Conveying this broader view of the library media program as defined by *Information Power: Building Partnerships for Learning* must be communicated throughout the planning process so that it can be clearly reflected in the mission, goals, and objectives of the school's library media program.

Teachers and administrators must become aware of the importance of information literacy as the means to students' success in the future; to understand the value and necessity of teaching students the critical and creative thinking skills that enable them to use information; and to acknowledge that the information curriculum is an integral part of the basic instructional program from earliest elementary grades through senior high.

Your leadership in communicating these concepts cannot be overemphasized. You must collaborate closely and continually with teachers and administrators in identifying where information curriculum proficiencies are already included in the curriculum, which proficiencies have not been included, and where and how the information curriculum can be most effectively introduced.

What do you see as the emerging priorities in education in your school? What role does your library media program play in supporting these priorities? What is the program's most important function? Spend some time thinking about these questions. You must be able to articulate your vision of the changing role of the library media program to others in order to gain their support. Write down some key words or phases below. These key words or phrases will help you focus on important aspects of your program and will influence your early decisions about the planning process. Your ideas will form the basis of a draft mission statement that you can share with others.

Determining your mission is the first essential step in the planning process. We will provide further guidance to help you develop a draft mission statement in subsequent sections, but it is important to jot down your initial thoughts at this time.

You have just taken the first step in the planning process. Several more steps are necessary before you are ready to begin working with others in the process, but you must not omit these initial steps. Time spent now putting your own thoughts on paper will enable you to effectively work with others and to rally the support and assistance you need. The following questions serve as your guide through this preliminary phase.

What are your purposes for planning? What do you want to change? to add? to support or maintain? (Write down your ideas.)

_____

_____

_____

_____

What products do you expect from your planning effort? How will the results be communicated? To which groups?

_____

_____

_____

_____

Who should be involved in the planning process? Who are the key persons in your school community whose support is essential if your planning is to bring about successful results? Principal, teacher, parent, student, custodian? Write down their names and the reasons that they must be involved.

Name _____

Reason _____

Name _____

Reason _____

Name _____

Reason _____

Name _____

Reason _____

Name _____

Reason _____

Name _____

Reason _____

If a planning process is to be successful in your school building, support from your principal is *vital*. If your principal's name is not on the list above, add it! You cannot successfully initiate this planning process without the principal's support. If there is a major critic of your program, add this person's name. The planning process offers an excellent opportunity to involve this person in a positive experience and increase his or her understanding of your program. There are other important persons to consider, such as key department chairs, grade-level chairs, resource teachers, special-subject teachers, informal instructional leaders, influential parents, district library media and curriculum staff members, and state department consultants.

Now, look again at your list and decide which individuals should be actively involved on your Planning Committee. Star their names. Do you have a cross section of teachers, administrators, and community representatives? Will these individuals be influential in effecting changes that will result from the planning process? How can you help them understand how this planning process for the library media program will contribute to the overall improvement of the educational program of the school? What strategies must you develop to communicate to each individual your vision of the library media program? How will you convince them of the importance and value of planning? Consider these questions.

Who can help me persuade these essential people to become involved in this planning process?

_____

_____

_____

What do I expect from the planning committee members? What will be their specific responsibilities in the planning process?

_____

_____

_____

_____

What criteria will we use to assess the effectiveness of the current library media program?

_____

_____

_____

How much time will be required for the planning process? for the library staff? for the Planning Committee members? for other members of the school community?

_____

_____

_____

What resources are required to support the planning effort?

_____

_____

_____

When will each phase of the planning process be completed?

_____

_____

_____

How will the activities, results, and recommendations from the planning process be evaluated? by whom? at what point?

_____

_____

_____

By answering these questions, you have developed the basis for your planning process. You have determined your strategies for communicating the purposes of the planning process, you have outlined your timeline, and you have considered how to persuade the key players to work with you. Together, you and the Planning Committee will oversee the planning process that will result in the library media program that best serves your school—which you will always want to refer to as "our," not "my," school, "our" library media center, and "our" program. You have now completed the initial steps in the planning process. You have:

- examined your current perceptions of the emerging priorities in education and the changing role of the library media center

- examined your concept of the library media program in relationship to these changing roles and emerging priorities

- identified the key concepts of your vision for your program

- identified your existing library supporters

- identified potential members of your Planning Committee

- developed strategies for existing supporters to help you persuade these key players to participate in the planning effort

- created a feasible timeline for committee tasks and deadlines

- developed a list of possible criteria needed by the committee to assess the effectiveness of the current program.

Planning the First Committee Meeting

Congratulations! You have now completed the preliminary tasks in examining your school library media program. You have identified your committee members, contacted them, and established their commitment to the importance of a quality school library media program. Now, it's time to bring them together to begin their work.

What do you want to accomplish during the first meeting of the Planning Committee? What can you logically expect to accomplish? How long will the meeting last? Your agenda for the first meeting of the Library Media Program Planning Committee might include a preliminary discussion of the items listed below. However, in-depth discussions of these issues will probably require one or more meetings later in the planning cycle.

1. Vision of the Library Media Program
   The first meeting offers a good opportunity to share your vision and encourage discussion.

2. Outline of the Planning Process
   Why plan? Who's involved? How do we do it? How do we evaluate the results? You considered these questions in your preparation for the planning process. Now, is the time to share your thoughts and ideas.

3. Timeline for Planning Process Committee Activities
   What are our priorities? What are our tasks and deadlines? Are they reasonable? The first meeting is a good time for committee members to share their ideas, concerns, and expectations about the planning process. It is also the time to establish the sense of teamwork that will be important throughout the upcoming months. The last item on the agenda should be the schedule and plan for the next meeting during which the committee will begin the group process of developing the mission statement for the library media program.

You have a responsibility as the leader of the Planning Committee to provide appropriate background materials. Consider giving each member a copy of *Information Power: Building Partnerships for Learning*. If you don't want to provide the entire book, plan to provide at least an abstract, an executive summary, the principles that are included in most chapters or a copy of *Information Literacy Standards for Student Learning*. A written statement of your library media program philosophy, as well as a copy of the school's philosophy, will be helpful to the planning committee. These two documents should be examined by the committee members to identify similar concerns and to correlate their content in those areas of similarity.

Be sure to distribute the agenda and appropriate documents well before your first meeting. Your committee members will appreciate the opportunity to prepare for the meeting. It is important to get your first meeting off to a good start and to convey to the group that you are interested in making the best use of their time and ideas.

At subsequent meetings, you may want to raise with the entire group additional questions you considered individually during your preparation for the planning process. Discussion by the group may result in solutions to difficult situations, e.g., budgeting for nonprofessional staff, coverage for mandated classroom teacher release time, or the lock-step scheduling of library instruction classes in elementary school settings.

Developing Your Mission Statement

The planning process is now well underway. The next step is for you to complete the preparation necessary to work with the Planning Committee in developing the mission for the library media program in your school. You, as the library media specialist, are responsible for articulating a vision of the program and leading the Planning Committee through a brainstorming process that will ultimately transform that vision into a statement of purpose. In preparing for this process, think about the philosophy of your school district and determine the influence it will have on the direction of the library media program. Write down the major concepts of the school district's philosophy that apply to your program.

_____

_____

_____

Answering the following questions about the library media program in your district may help you work with the Planning Committee in shaping your mission statement.

Why does the library media program exist?

_____

_____

_____

How does it contribute to student learning?

_____

_____

_____

How can it better contribute to student learning?

_____

_____

_____

What are its unique responsibilities?

_____

_____

_____

_____

_____

What are the roles of the library media specialist and how must they change?

_____

_____

_____

_____

_____

What is the role of the classroom teacher and how must it change?

_____

_____

_____

Record key words and phrases which arise from your answers to these questions.

_____

_____

_____

Now that you have done some preliminary thinking about the mission of your program, you are ready to begin working with the Planning Committee to draft the mission statement. In working with the committee, the first step is to reach consensus about the purpose of the library media program in your school. Use the above questions about the mission of your library media program to guide the Planning Committee's discussion. During this discussion you need to make certain that key ideas are recorded.

Brainstorming is an effective technique for generating ideas in a group. Here are a few guidelines for brainstorming, which you may find helpful.

- Identify a recorder. You need someone to keep track of ideas for future reference. You will be busy leading the process and keeping everyone involved.

- Record the ideas on newsprint or overhead transparency film. Consider having someone enter the notes into a computer to record greater detail for later use. Everyone must be able to read and respond to the ideas during the session.
- Remember that all ideas are acceptable during the brainstorming process. The intent is to generate ideas; evaluating them will come later.

After the group discussion or brainstorming process, the group must reach consensus on the needed elements for the mission statement. Record the key phrases. They are the foundation for the draft statement of your mission.

The mission statement should be brief—no more than two to five sentences. the preliminary wording of the statement can be assigned to one person, but the Planning Committee should review the draft and revise it as needed.

Draft Mission Statement

_____

_____

_____

_____

_____

After a preliminary mission statement is written, the committee may want to share the draft with the faculty, the student body, the school administration, the board of education, and parent groups. Sharing in this manner serves as an awareness-building activity while helping the committee to define the program mission. Revisions may be made following a review of comments made by these groups.

Revised Mission Statement

_____

_____

_____

_____

_____

_____

When consensus has been reached on the mission of your school library media program, it is appropriate to begin developing goals and objectives.

Developing Goals and Objectives

Now that you have defined your mission, you are ready to construct goals and objectives for your program. Although this task will be a responsibility of the Planning Committee, it may be wise for you to work with one or two members of the committee to prepare draft goals and objectives for presentation to the entire committee.

To create appropriate and realistic goals and objectives that will serve as a guide for achieving the vision articulated in your mission statement, you must understand your school community. Several types of information may be needed to gain this understanding, most of which are readily available in district reports.

- Demographic data: e.g., age and sex distribution in the community
- Socioeconomic factors: ethnic background; primary languages spoken in the homes; family structures; educational level and expectations of parents and other community members; and characteristics of the at-risk student populations
- Curricular information: ability levels, subjects taught, types of class assignments, textbook adoptions, learning and teaching styles, curriculum guides, and plans for new courses or changing courses.

It will be necessary to work with school administrators, curriculum directors, and others to collect some of these data for use by the Planning Committee. Other data may be collected informally through a "walkabout"—looking at your environment, as if for the first time, in an effort to gather impressions about its social milieu. After you and the members of the Planning Committee working with you on this task have gathered and analyzed this information, you will be ready to begin working with the entire committee in developing goals and objectives. The following quote from the Public Library Association's *Planning and Role Setting for Public Libraries,* published by the American Library Association in 1987, puts the task of constructing goals and objectives into perspective:

The planning process is like a funnel. The beginning of the process is like the wide end of the funnel, open to all kinds of possibilities. As planning decisions are made, the funnel narrows. (p. 43)

Goals and objectives serve to narrow the funnel as they identify areas of activity most important for the school library media program and as they establish performance targets within those areas.

In the planning process, goals and objectives serve to:
- guide the actions of decision makers, including the library media specialists
- provide the rationale for developing program activities
- inform students, teachers, and administrators about the elements of the school's media program that the Planning Committee specifically wants to emphasize
- assist you and future planning committees in assessing the effectiveness of the program as well as demonstrating accountability.

Goals are broad statements describing a desired condition. They may be stated as ideals toward which you will work over the next three to five years. Goals most effectively communicate the mission of the library media program when they are stated from the perspective of the student learner, although they may also be expressed in terms of the library media program.

Example: (goal expressed in learner outcomes)
All students are effective users of ideas and information.

Example: (goal expressed in program outcomes)
The library media program provides the materials and services necessary for all students to become effective users of ideas and information.

Now, using key terms from your mission statement, prepare two or three goals that express desired outcomes of the mission.

_____

_____

_____

_____

It is important that the mission and goals of the library media program are understood and adopted by the entire school district. It may be appropriate for the Planning Committee to share them at a school board meeting and/or at a district inservice meeting for all faculty.

Objectives

Objectives are short-term statements that describe the results of specific actions. Objectives translate the goal into achievable steps in the quarter-, semester-, or year-long planning cycle. Objectives begin with an action verb and must be measurable so that it is possible to determine how well they have been met.

Examples of action verbs include:

formulate	write	discuss	compare
contrast	identify	solve	design
construct	organize	instruct	use
select	differentiate	evaluate	define
prepare	classify	manipulate	explain
create	analyze	predict	produce

Objectives may be expressed in terms of student and faculty outcomes. Using the goal "All students are effective users of ideas and information," related objectives might include the following:

Students will:
- analyze a search question to determine key words.
- use a variety of indexes to locate citations for potentially useful information.

Teachers will:
- design assignments that require students to use multiple sources.

The library media specialist will:
- instruct fifth grade students in the use of a variety of indexes.

Obviously, complete coverage of the goal stated above would require a wide range of objectives dealing with all facets of the search process, as well as the organization and preparation of a finished product suitable for the assignment. The examples provided are limited to skills related to the use of indexes.

Select one of your goal statements and break it into two or three achievable steps that will move you toward the goal. These steps are objectives.

_____

_____

_____

_____

_____

Think about a reasonable timeline within the organization of your school calendar. Are these objective statements achievable in a quarter, semester, or school year?

_____

_____

_____

How would an observer know when an objective is completed? Did you describe observable or measurable actions so that this objective can be evaluated?

_____

_____

_____

Revise these objectives as necessary and then prepare additional objectives for your remaining goal statements.

Additional Tips

The long-range planning cycle typically lasts from three to five years. Your goal statements should remain essentially the same over that period of time. Your objectives, however, may change during each quarter, semester, or year, depending on your timeline and how the completion of each of the objectives, or achievable steps moves the library media program closer to goals agreed upon by the Planning Committee and adopted by the school.

If this is the first systematic planning process you have undertaken in your school, you will probably want to identify only three to five goals and two or three objectives for each goal. Engaging in a systematic planning process is in itself a learning process for all participants. Limiting the number of goals and objectives will help to ensure that both your plan and your Planning Committee will be successful.

Collecting Needed Information

Data gathering takes place throughout the planning process. It is an essential component because it provides documentation that either validates or invalidates the assumptions made about your program. Data gathering and the resulting analysis serve several purposes by helping to:

- describe a program as it is (providing baseline data)
- document or provide support for an idea
- describe changes that occur during the implementation of an idea
- identify strengths and weaknesses
- evaluate progress
- raise awareness levels concerning a problem, condition, or solution, i.e., a tool in public relations

It is easy to make two incorrect assumptions about data gathering:

1. Objective data are the only acceptable data.
2. Data must be collected over a long period of time.

Subjective or intuitive data from staff and users may be just as useful as objective data because they provide a broader picture of the library media program. Analysis of research methods has shown that samples of an activity can reflect an accurate picture of the activity over time—i.e., circulation statistics need not be collected every day of the year, but selected samples throughout the year can reflect the total year.

As the Planning Committee begins to define the types and amount of baseline data needed to assess the current program, and those that will be needed for future evaluation purposes, consider a number of options. A number of simple data-gathering techniques can be used in a variety of ways, for several purposes:

- Tallies and counts (circulation statistics; patron use of catalogs and indexes; number of planning session with teachers; interlibrary loans)
- Ratios (materials used compared to the total collection; reference successes as compared to failures; teacher conferences per number of teachers)
- Schedules and calendars (class visits, special programs)
- Logs and anecdotal records (formal and informal planning sessions with teachers; curriculum meetings attended; classes taught in conjunction with content area specialists; reader's guidance and individual instruction)
- Observations (number of students using the library media center during a specific period; purposes for use; availability of collection)
- Products (curriculum guides, instructional materials, working papers, workshops directed)

As the Planning Committee develops plans for collecting relevant data, remember that the purpose of the collection is to gauge how well your program meets the needs of the students and staff. Data gathering is merely a means to an end, and it should not become the primary focus of the planning effort.

After you identify the types of data you need to collect, you must construct a plan for data gathering. A major consideration must be the time and difficulty of the activity. You and the Planning Committee must determine who will be responsible for and will oversee the data collection; who will construct the timeline; how the data will be tabulated and analyzed; who will perform the data analysis; and how the results will be used. The plan must indicate the resources necessary to accomplish the task. If external resources such as money or supplies are required for data collection, the Planning Committee must enlist administrative support. Of course, since you have already involved your principal and other key administrators in the development of the planning process, such support should be readily available.

In addition to the data collecting techniques listed above, the use of interviews and properly prepared questionnaires may be helpful. Both of these data collection methods call for careful planning and construction. Neither method provides the information being sought when untested questions—worded without giving sufficient thought to possible ramifications or interpretations—are used.

Basic rules for construction of interviews and questionnaires include the following:
- determine the precise information that is needed
- decide whether answers will be supplied by the respondent or selected from options provided
- make certain that the people being queried are the right ones to ask—that they have the interest and information
- express questions as clearly and simply as possible
- avoid words that might be subject to different interpretations, as well as jargon
- avoid using unnecessary words
- make certain all modifying descriptors needed to provide a reasonable basis for response are included—e.g., children defined by age group or grade level
- phrase questions so that truthful answers may be given freely; avoid questions that may be embarrassing, leading, or subject to socially acceptable responses
- avoid asking for personal opinion unless that is what is being sought
- provide a final open-ended response opportunity.

After the questions are formulated, try them out on a few people who are representative of those being queried. Have them identify questions that cause difficulty for them, are fuzzy in meaning, or may be interpreted in more than one way. Modify these questions and retest, if necessary, before using them to gather data.

When conducting fact-finding interviews, a friendly atmosphere must be established. The questions to be asked should be written down and used consistently. Recording responses, either by writing notes or using a tape recorder, can be intimidating to the person being interviewed. Try to be as unobtrusive as possible in the note-taking process. When responses are recorded following an interview, errors of omission are frequent. If this technique of recording is used, plan to complete the report as soon as possible, following the interview.

For an interview to be successful, the interviewer must think like the person being interviewed. Adequate response time must be given to get full answers. The interviewer must be cautious about implying answers through facial expressions, registering surprise or shock at disclosures, being patronizing, or creating defensiveness on the part of the person being interviewed.

Both interviews and questionnaires should be as brief as possible, consistent with the intended level of coverage. Omit trivial or unnecessary queries. Sometimes the categories planned for data analysis must be modified in light of the responses. A final reminder—be sure to ensure the anonymity of the respondents, and be sure to report to them the results of the survey.

Developing Action Plans

The data you have collected present a snapshot of the library media program as it now exists. As you look at the picture of the program, notice the areas that are bold and clear—the areas where your program seems to mirror your mission statement. Note also the areas that are fuzzy, those where there seems to be no clear evidence that the goals and objectives you have identified are being met.

The next task for you and your Planning Committee is to clarify the picture—to identify the activities or steps that are necessary to develop the picture and move from what is to what should be, i.e., to realize your goals or implement your objectives. To identify possible activities, the Planning Committee again will probably want to use a brainstorming approach. Remember that in brainstorming, all suggestions—whether practical or irrational—are accepted without evaluation on the first round. When all the creative solutions have been offered, you may want to look at the list you have made and then identify several actions in each area that have real potential for implementation.

Star those ideas that are possible steps in your action plan. Some changes will fall within the jurisdiction of the library media specialist; some will require a directive from a school administrator or a change in board of education policy; some will require funding and have budgetary implications that will take time and the action of others to implement. As you examine these possibilities, check to be sure that the suggested activities will move your program toward a specific objective or goal. (A good way to do this is to try to predict the outcome of the activity—and to identify a way to measure that outcome.)

Sometimes difficult decisions must be made as new activities or plans of action are examined in terms of their impact on existing resources and programs. For each activity your Planning Committee will want to consider carefully the following questions:

- Does the activity relate to the statements of goals and objectives?
- What physical and human resources will be required to carry out the activity?
- Are the necessary resources available or will existing resources need to be reallocated or reorganized?
- What will the positive or negative impact be on current activities and services? Will something need to be reduced or dropped? Is this wise?
- Do the library media staff members have the competencies necessary to carry out the activity? If not, how can these be acquired? Within what time frame?
- Must staff time be reallocated to implement the new activity? Is this feasible?

When you have considered these questions and selected the best activities or steps, it will be necessary to transfer your ideas to the Action Plan worksheet, which ties the activities to the appropriate objectives and goals. Note that as you place your action steps in sequence, you will need to:

- identify the resources that will be necessary to implement each step
- list the individual or group that will be primarily responsible for taking the action

- note when the step is to be started
- anticipate completion of the activity
- decide what data collection will be necessary to document progress toward your goal or objective.

Repeat this clarification process for each action plan. As you prepare each plan, reconsider the time and resource allocations necessary. When you have completed each plan, consider the following questions:

- Do your action steps mesh together?
- Are the expectations of staff, teachers, and/or students reasonable?
- Are there timelines that need to be reworked?

Now, take one more look at your mission statement. Is the mission reflected in each part of your action plan? Does your vision of the school library media program shine through? Are you and your Planning Committee members excited about taking the action steps?

If the answers to these questions are yes, then you're ready to celebrate! If the answers are no, modifications must be made. (You may need to reorganize or reword a bit to be sure the mission statement, goals, objectives, and action steps or strategies are clear and concisely stated.)

The next step is to share your entire plan with the school community, the school board, administrators, teachers, students, and parents. Your Planning Committee members may even want to help you plan a celebration to share your vision of the future! It is essential that the plan be shared, understood, and accepted by key leaders in your school. Working together, the total school community can ensure that the vision for the library media program can become a reality.

Evaluating the Library Media Program

The committee's work is never done...

An integral part of the planning process is regular evaluation. Unfortunately, this phase is often neglected or ignored. Have you ever wondered why carefully made plans are sometimes unsuccessful? One reason may be that the plans are not carefully monitored. Your leadership is crucial during this phase of the planning process. The committee members have worked long and hard on the plan. They may be tired and ready to end the process quickly, but you must make certain this final phase is not forgotten.

The Planning Committee must develop a process to ensure the systematic and regular evaluation of the progress of the plan. The members of the committee may decide to serve as the monitoring group in the evaluation process, or another group may be established. If a different committee is desired, some members of the original Planning Committee (other than you) should be encouraged to participate during the first year of implementation and evaluation to provide consistency and continuity.

The selection of evaluative criteria to measure and monitor the progress toward achieving goals and objectives will be based upon your plan. You may want to begin the Planning Committee's discussion of the evaluation process by raising these questions:

- What proportion of the total school population (students and staff) is being reached?
- What identifiable subgroups are being reached? in what ways? with what frequency?
- With what frequency and effectiveness does the library media specialist participate in instructional planning with teachers?
- How effectively can students use information resources to meet specific learning objectives?
- With what frequency and effectiveness do teachers use library media resources and activities to accomplish classroom objectives?
- How well are the library media program's objectives being met?

Principles 5 and 6 in Chapter 6 of *Information Power: Building Partnerships for Learning* discuss the importance of assessment and long-range planning and list goals that will assist in developing your plan. In addition, you may want to recommend other published sources on evaluation to the committee such as those listed in the bibliography at the end of this booklet. The evaluation process grows out of your plan, and the criteria by which you will judge your success must be established prior to implementation of the plan. You must clearly identify how you will know if your plan is a success, otherwise this whole process may be a failure!

Remember—this evaluation process becomes the first step in reviewing your mission, goals, and objectives for the next planning cycle. Planning is an ongoing process, but from now on a much easier one, because you have developed the techniques!

Your leadership in guiding the Planning Committee through the process is critical. You have a number of responsibilities. You must:

- carry the vision
- organize a clearly defined planning timeline
- provide ways to collect needed information
- prepare implementation strategies for committee recommendations
- set up a regular evaluation process *and*
- be a cheerleader when other members appear hesitant or overwhelmed.

Throughout the planning process, it is also vital that you continue to provide a high level of library media service to your school community. *Planning is critical, but it must not be done at the expense of your current program!*

One Final Word

We hope that this guide to planning has been helpful. Planning the direction of your school's library media program in a systematic manner, implementing that plan, and then evaluating its progress is a challenging, but rewarding experience. Use *Information Power: Building Partnerships for Learning*, this guide, the Action Plan and Planning Chart which follow to develop a library media program that will enable your students to become effective and efficient users of information throughout their lives. Empower them! If you need additional help in the planning process or implementing the recommendation in the new guidelines, contact the American Association of School Librarians. We are planning publications, pre-conferences, conference sessions, and workshops on the new guidelines. Let us know how we can help you.

So here you are, standing by the circulation desk, with *Information Power: Building Partnerships for Learning* in one hand and your completed plan in the other. What a sense of pride you feel as you think about the participation of the Planning Committee, the enthusiasm of your teachers and administrators as they adopted the plan. Your vision has become a shared vision, changed here and there throughout the planning process, but resulting in a library media program that will help students and faculty members be effective users of ideas and information.

Sample Action Plan

GOAL # 1

All students are effective users of ideas and information.

Objective:

Teachers will design assignments that require students to use multiple sources.

Target Groups

School district decision-makers, school boards, general public, parents, principals, teachers, students.

Strategies

What? (the obstacles)

Describe the program as it is (providing baseline data).

Document or provide support for an idea.

Identify strength and weaknesses.

Where?

Provide rationale for developing program activities.

Inform students, teachers and administrators about the school media program and that the planning committee wants to emphasize.

When?

Give dates when each phase of plan is to be completed

Who? (is going to do it?)

District Library Media Coordinators, Building Level Media Specialists

Be specific. Name names. Give specific responsibilities to individuals.

How? (the message)

Raise awareness levels concerning a problem, condition or solution.

What is the specific message that the target group is to receive that will bring about the desired change?

Communication Tools

Given all of the above, what communication tools will be most appropriate for the target group? e.g. cosponsored events, programs, presentations, video, PowerPoint®, promotional materials, publications. (Groups small enough for one-on-one communication will be the most effective.)

Evaluation

Measurable objectives mean that activities have to be put in place to ensure measurements are taken. If you can't measure it, you probably shouldn't be doing it.

Action Plan

GOAL # _____

Objective:

Target Groups

Strategies

What? (the obstacles)

Where?

When?

Who? (is going to do it?)

How? (the message)

Communication Tools

Evaluation

Sample

Planning Chart

With Progress Notes and Completion Dates

Objective	Target Groups	Person Responsible	Progress Notes	Date Completed
Teachers will design assignments that will require students to use multiple resources.	Classroom teachers Building principals	District Coordinator Building Level Library Media Specialists	Logs of formal and informal planing sessions are being maintained. Tallies of student use of resources are being made.	In Progress
The library media program provides the materials and services necessary for all students to become effective users of ideas and information.	Building and district administrators, school board, parents, teachers	District Coordinator Building Level Library Media Specialists	Tally of unanswered inquiries. Evaluations of collaboratively planned units. Curriculum Map Collection Map	In Progress December 1998 June 1998

Planning Chart
With Progress Notes and Completion Dates

Objective	Target Groups	Person Responsible	Progress Notes	Date Completed

School Library Media Program
Assessment Rubric
for the 21st Century:
A Self-Assessment Tool
for School Districts

Prepared by the
Assessment Rubric Subcommittee
Teaching for Learning Task Force
American Association of School Librarians

Assessment Rubric Committee

AASL Teaching for Learning Task Force

Barbara Stripling, Chairperson
Director of Instruction and Information Services
Fayetteville Public Schools
Fayetteville, Arkansas

Assessment Rubric Subcommittee

Carol Kroll, Chairperson
Supervisor
Nassau School Library System
Nassau BOCES
Massapequa Park, New York

Vi Harada
Associate Professor
University of Hawaii
Graduate School of Library and Information Studies
Honolulu, Hawaii

Dorna Perrson
Library Media Specialist
Fairfield Public Schools
Fairfield, Connecticut

Sheila Salmon
Senior Vice President (retired)
New Visions for Public Schools
New York, New York

Introduction

Rubric Development

This national document was created by members of the American Association of School Librarians (AASL). It has as its roots the "Rubric for the Assessment of the School Library Media Program," created in February 1996 by a group of Colorado library media specialists working with the Colorado State Library. The group included Eugene Hainer, Colorado State Library; Kay Evatz and Marcie Haloin, Adams 12 School District; Jody Gehrig and Yvonne Jost, Denver Public Schools; Deb Kirk, Weld County School District #6; Billie Wolter and Christette Soderberg, Jefferson County Public Schools; Judy MacDonald and Marcene Amand, Poudre Valley Public Schools.

Barbara Stripling built on the Colorado document and integrated the Target Indicators from *Information Power: Building Partnerships for Learning* (Chicago: American Library Association, 1998) into the Rubric. In 1997 Barbara worked with a group of library media specialists from the Nassau School Library System (NSLS) in New York State to gain input from the field.

In 1998 Sharon Coatney, President of AASL from 1998-99, asked Barbara Stripling to chair the Teaching for Learning Task Force. A subcommittee, under the leadership of Carol Kroll, was formed to bring the Rubric to fruition. The subcommittee significantly altered the original document using key elements from *Information Power: Building Partnerships for Learning* and leaving in place the Target Indicators. The Rubric was field tested in New York by 67 library media specialists from 56 school districts within the Nassau School Library System and New York City library media specialists affiliated with New Visions for Public Schools. Students at the University of Hawaii School of Information Studies offered suggestions. During a six month period discussion centered on determinants of quality media programs. The emphasis moved from the library media specialists to the library media program and then to policies in place in the school district.

The Rubric was then tested by central office administrators in three school districts, and their comments were incorporated into the document.

Members of the Teaching for Learning Task Force discussed the Rubric via the task force electronic discussion list and readied it for submission to the AASL Board of Directors during the 1999 ALA Annual Conference in New Orleans. The Board unanimously approved the Rubric with the decision to publish it as a significant piece in the implementation of *Information Power: Building Partnerships for Learning.*

District Policy Determines Quality of Library Media Program

The quality of library media programs is dependent on policies in place in a particular school district. Districts are urged to adopt policies that support library media centers as collaborative centers of teaching and learning. District policies determine when students can have access to school library media center resources, budget size, staffing levels, technology infrastructure, facility design, opportunities for collaboration between classroom teachers and the library media specialist, support for staff development, and processes for teaching and learning. Policies that strengthen the library media program must be in place for the learning needs of students and teachers to be met.

District Use of the Rubric

The Target Indicators outline elements of a school library media program. The building principal, along with the school library media specialist, can use the Rubric as a tool to assess the quality of the school's programs. Short and long range goals can be identified to upgrade services. The Rubric was designed to help the entire school staff and community members gain a deeper understanding of the elements of a successful school library media learning environment.

Completion of the Rubric

When the library media specialist and the principal work together to complete the Rubric, strengths and needs of the program, and how the school's policies impact it, become clear. The goal setting activity supports change. Most programs will be at the Basic level. With realistic goal-setting activities, elements of the school library media program can move from Basic to Proficient to perhaps Exemplary.

Scenarios Describing Programs at Each Level

School Policies result in a library media program at the Basic Level

This is a positive model where all children have access to the library media center. The library media program is developed and information skills are taught by the library media specialist with some input from the classroom teachers related to classroom themes and/or curriculum. There is a collection that is responsive to the curriculum and student interests. Some technology exists. The climate is conducive to learning. There is a full-time library media specialist and some support staff. Consistent funding is at a maintenance level. The facility is large enough to accommodate a class and a half with sufficient shelving for the collection and appropriate furniture and wiring. In the elementary school there is a reading and storytelling area. The library media specialist is in control of the student work, directing all activities and assessments.

School Policies result in a library media program at the Proficient Level

This positive model provides flexible access to the library media center during the school day. Collaborative planning takes place with some of the staff, with some school-wide programming, and with some parent participation. The collection has a depth in both subject matter and format. The library media center has a network with multiple access to the Internet. There are written guidelines. An inviting climate encourages students and teachers to make frequent use of the library media center. The full-time professional staff is supported by a full-time support staff. An adequate budget is in place to support the curricular and personal interests of learners. The library media program is written into fundraising proposals, bonds, etc. and is incorporated into the capital outlay plan. Space is provided for two classes with additional space for small groups and individuals. Some learning is student initiated with small group and individual teaching and assessment by both the library media specialist and the teacher.

School Policies result in a library media program at the Exemplary Level

This positive model provides flexible access to the library media center extending beyond the school day. The collaboratively planned program is central to teaching and learning; is multifaceted; encourages independent learners; and reaches beyond the doors of the school. The collection extends into the classrooms for both print and electronic resources. The library is networked within the school, the district, and the community. There is a continuous flow of students and teachers between classrooms and the library media center to meet classroom and personal needs. Staffing follows usage so that high usage results in additional professional and support staff. Funding supports a large, diverse, in-depth, school-wide collection. The library media program is written into fundraising proposals, bonds, etc., and is incorporated into the capital outlay plan. Multiple classes and small groups can be accommodated with production space, presentation space, and flexibility in design. The library media specialist models teaching techniques to teachers and students with students encouraged to be independent learners.

School Library Media Program Assessment

This document is designed to help schools upgrade school library media programs. It should be used as a self-assessment tool and action plan in each school. Administrators and library media specialists are encouraged to work together to complete the assessment rubric. Use the responses and comments noted during completion of the assessment rubric to identify goals, the process of achieving them, and district policies that will be re-examined or written. Actions taken to achieve the goals should help to move library media services from one level to another, i.e., Basic to Proficient within particular Target Indicators and to improve teaching and learning.

Library media specialists should work with the library media program advisory committee or principal to identify one or two immediate goals and one or two long-range goals and to determine timetables for implementation.

When identifying goals, consider the following issues:
- Budget
- Partners
- Time allocation
- Professional development needs
- Implications for collection
- Implication for staff

Some goals will require a minimum of attention to these issues; others much more.

School Library Media Program Assessment

Prepared by the American Association of School Librarians
Teaching for Learning Task Force Subcommittee

Please check (✓) one that applies for each Target Indicator. Leave blank if you are not yet at the basic level. Write notes in the comments section to use in setting goals.

A. Teaching and Learning

Target Indicators	Basic	Proficient	Exemplary	Comments
1. Information Literacy Standards are integrated into content learning.	☐ Students learn to use library materials in the context of classroom content. Library skills are locational skills or how to find information.	☐ The library media program provides essential support to the curriculum. Students learn information literacy skills, which extend beyond location to analysis, evaluation, and use of information through collaborative efforts of teachers and the library media specialist.	☐ The library media program is a catalyst for intellectual inquiry. Students learn to incorporate information literacy skills into their work and become proactive users of information and resources.	
2. Collaborative planning is modeled and promoted.	☐ Discussions take place between the library media specialist and teacher regarding lessons and the curriculum.	☐ Some teachers and the library media specialist collaboratively plan and teach curriculum units.	☐ The school schedule ensures time for the teachers and the library media specialist to regularly meet at common planning times, to plan instructional units, learning strategies, and activities. The library media specialist helps build a coordinated instructional program.	
3. Curriculum development is modeled and promoted.	☐ The library media program reflects the curriculum and curriculum guides and/or information are provided to teachers and library media specialist.	☐ School policies enable the library media specialist to participate in building and district-wide curriculum meetings and share knowledge and resources.	☐ The district encourages the library media specialist to work collaboratively with administrators and teachers in planning, developing, and writing curriculum.	
4. Effective teaching is modeled and promoted.	☐ The library media specialist participates in directing activities and assessment of student work.	☐ Teaching is generally facilitative. The teacher and/or library media specialist may prescribe the strategies, research questions or assessment products to be used.	☐ Teaching is facilitative, collaborative, and creative. Reflection and authentic assessment are built into all instructional units.	

A. Teaching and Learning

Target Indicators	Basic	Proficient	Exemplary	Comments
5. Students are engaged in reading, writing, speaking, viewing, and listening for enjoyment, enrichment, and understanding.	☐ The library media program regularly promotes reading, viewing, and listening.	☐ The library media program offers special literacy related events that motivate students to view, listen, write, or speak on their own or as part of classroom activities.	☐ The school-wide culture encourages viewing, reading, writing, speaking, and listening for the intrinsic rewards of learning, enrichment, and personal pleasure.	
6. Students with diverse learning abilities, styles, and needs are given support.	☐ The library media program reflects diverse learning abilities and collaborative methods to accommodate them.	☐ The library media specialist helps students to recognize and use their own learning styles.	☐ School-wide programs enable and encourage students to use their own learning styles, abilities, and needs to solve complex information problems and present their solutions in various formats.	
7. Inquiry is fostered.	☐ Library media specialists and/or teachers present choices for research and may determine research groups or partners. The library media specialist or teacher defines the resources to be used.	☐ Students are given an opportunity to select topics within a theme and the resources to be used. Students may select their research partner.	☐ Inquiry can take place by an individual or in a group. Students determine their own research needs and develop their own research strategies.	
8. Student achievement is assessed.	☐ The teacher assesses a product produced to fulfill an assignment.	☐ Demonstrations of student learning are assessed by the teacher and library media specialist using a teacher and library media specialist produced rubric. Students may also be assessed during presentations to peers.	☐ Student learning is assessed through student presentations to peers and adults, using student and teacher produced rubrics. Students may also present to professionals in the field of study.	

B. Information Access and Delivery

Target Indicators	Basic	Proficient	Exemplary	Comments
1. Physical access to information and resources provided.				
a. Facility	☐ The facility is large enough to accommodate a class with additional space for small groups for book selection or independent research. There is sufficient shelving for the collection, appropriate furniture, professional workspace, storage, and wiring. Elementary libraries have an area for storytelling.	☐ The facility is large enough to accommodate areas for large and small groups and individuals working simultaneously. There is ample shelving for the collection, appropriate furniture, professional workspace, storage, and wiring. Elementary libraries have an area for storytelling.	☐ Multiple classes and small groups can be accommodated. Production space, presentation space, and flexibility in design are provided in the library media center.	
b. Resources	☐ An online catalog and circulation system provides access to a collection supplemented by interlibrary loan.	☐ A library network provides students with access to a variety of information resources within the library and from their homes. Interlibrary loan is forwarded electronically within the region.	☐ The collection extends into classrooms for both print and electronic resources. The library is networked within the school, the district, and the community. Interlibrary loan is conducted throughout the state and beyond.	
2. A climate conducive to learning is provided.	☐ The learning community feels welcome and drawn to the inviting library media center.	☐ Some students frequently use the library media center on their own because the center is warm and inviting and students are able to work productively.	☐ Students consistently use the library media center on their own during and beyond the school day. The environment stimulates and supports productive and focused learning.	

B. Information Access and Delivery

Target Indicators	Basic	Proficient	Exemplary	Comments
3. Flexible and equitable access is ensured.	☐ Some flexible access is provided.	☐ Flexible access is proved during all hours that the school is in session	☐ Access to the library media center and its resources is fully flexible and available both during and beyond the school day.	
4. Collections support the curriculum and fulfill learning needs.	☐ The collection has been weeded, is up to date and responsive to curricular and patron needs. There are some multi-media and electronic resources.	☐ The collection is current and meets curricular and recreational needs. It is adequately balanced with resources in various formats to support diverse learning styles.	☐ The collection accommodates several classes working on comprehensive research. It is well-balanced with resources in all formats. The collection extends into the classrooms for both print and electronic resources.	
5. A commitment to the right of intellectual freedom is the foundation of the program.	☐ The library media program is fully committed to the concept of intellectual freedom.	☐ The library media program and staff support the concept of intellectual freedom and implement it through policies and practice.	☐ The entire school community supports intellectual freedom for all students and implements it through district policies and practices.	
6. Legal guidelines and professional ethics in information policies, procedures, and practices are in place.	☐ Written policies on information issues (selection, challenges, copyright, intellectual freedom, confidentiality, Internet acceptable use) have been developed and approved by the school and district.	☐ Written policies on information issues (selection, challenges, copyright, intellectual freedom, confidentiality, Internet acceptable use) have been developed and approved by the school and district.	☐ Written policies on information issues (selection, challenges, copyright, intellectual freedom, confidentiality, Internet acceptable use) have been developed and approved by the school and district.	

C. Program Administration

Target Indicators	Basic	Proficient	Exemplary	Comments
1. Staffing is at an appropriate level.	☐ The library media center is staffed with at least one full-time library media specialist and one part-time support staff.	☐ The library media center is staffed with at least one full-time library media specialist and at least a full-time support staff.	☐ Staffing follows usage so that high usage results in additional professional and support staff with at least one full-time library media specialist and one full-time support staff for every 500 students.	
2. Administration support is ongoing.	☐ The school administrator and central office administrators support the library media program. The school administrator makes time to meet with the library media specialist occasionally.	☐ The school administrator encourages teachers to integrate classroom learning into the library media program. School, department, and district administrators meet regularly with the library media specialists.	☐ The school administrator and central office administrators and library media specialists promote learning through inquiry. School department heads and district administrators meet regularly with the school library media specialists.	
3. Library operations are effective.	☐ Procedures exist to process, inventory, catalog, circulate, maintain, and weed the collection.	☐ Ample time and staff are allotted to implement library operation procedures.	☐ Staffing enables the library media specialist to focus on collaborative collection development and other professional responsibilities while supervising staff performing non-professional library operations.	
4. Comprehensive and collaborative program planning is in place.	☐ Strategic planning and goal setting exist.	☐ The school supports a team composed of library media specialist, teachers, parents, and the principal to determine current and future needs. A short-range plan for the library media program and resources is developed.	☐ Short and long range plans reflect a school-wide strategic planning process.	

C. Program Administration

Target Indicators	Basic	Proficient	Exemplary	Comments
5. There is an on-going assessment of the library media program.	☐ Assessment of the library media program is based on input criteria, such as the number of books added, the number of classes taught, circulation statistics, and the number of units designed.	☐ Teachers and students and the school community participate in the assessment of the library media program.	☐ An ongoing formal assessment process is central to community-wide planning that makes use of state and national assessment tools.	
6. Funding is sufficient.	☐ The library media program is funded at a level adequate to support the curriculum.	☐ A long-range budget includes funds for expansion. Grant and fundraising opportunities are sought to supplement the budget.	☐ Funding supports a large, diverse, in-depth, school-wide collection. Bond issues, grants, school fundraising, and business partnerships supplement the budget.	
7. There is ongoing staff development for teachers, administrators, and other members of the learning community.				
a. Learning community	☐ Professional resources are used by the faculty. The library media program provides individual assistance to teachers in using technology and designing instruction.	☐ The school provides opportunities for the library media specialist to organize and facilitate some formal professional development instruction.	☐ The school's strategic plan includes time for the library media specialist to coordinate many professional development opportunities including technology and inquiry.	

C. Program Administration

Target Indicators	Basic	Proficient	Exemplary	Comments
b. Library media specialist	☐ The library media specialist is encouraged to occasionally attend professional development conferences and courses. The library media specialist participates in a local professional organization.	☐ The library media specialist is encouraged to attend professional development opportunities and to share new ideas with the school and district. The library media specialist is an active member of a statewide professional organization.	☐ With the district's support the library media specialist organizes and coordinates workshops, models instructional strategies and coaches other teachers. The library media specialist takes a leadership role in professional organizations.	
8. The mission, goals, functions, and impact of the library media program are communicated.				
a. Sharing opportunities	☐ The district provides opportunity for library media specialists to meet occasionally to discuss district concerns, policy, procedures, and services.	☐ The district provides opportunity for library media specialists to meet regularly.	☐ The district encourages library media specialists to meet at least monthly.	
b. General Communication	☐ Time is allocated for the library media specialist to communicate the issues and successes of the library media program to the principal and parents.	☐ The district encourages the library media specialist to develop and maintain a library Web site and community newsletter, to contribute to local publications, and to advocate for school library media programs with public officials.	☐ Recognized in the district as a master teacher, the library media specialist publishes in national periodicals and Web sites, applies for recognition awards, receives visitations from other communities and reports at school board meetings regarding school library media services.	

Glossary of Terms Used in Assessment Rubric

Authentic Assessment

Evaluating learning by requiring students to demonstrate mastery in a "real life context." This may take the form of a portfolio which is a collection of work in progress, logs, writing samples, finished products, and other selected pieces that give a whole picture of students' progress. Authentic assessment is concerned with the process of learning in addition to measuring the mastery of content.

Challenged Material Policy

A district policy that provides for the review of any resource about which concerns have been raised. (See Selection Policy)

Collaborative Planning

In preparation for a class visit to the library media center, the library media specialist and the teacher(s) involved plan the students' assignments; assign responsibility for teaching the relevant skills; determine student activities and the content of the final product; and assess the process and results.

Collection Development

The process of building a library media center collection of resources in all formats including, but not limited to, book, electronic database, CD-ROM, and video to support all areas of the curriculum, individual research and a broad knowledge of the world's literature. In developing a collection, the library media specialist must take into consideration student and parent needs as well as the needs of the various professionals in the school community.

Facilitative Teaching

A model of teaching that strives to help students understand their own learning needs and "coaches" or guides them toward independent learning. The phrases "guide on the side" and "sage on the stage" are used to contrast the facilitative learning method to the lecture method.

Flexible Access

A library media center schedule that is arranged by the library media specialist in consultation with classroom teachers. Flexible access provides opportunities for individual students, small groups, and classes to visit the library media center when there is a need. Scheduling time for whole class visits vary from week to week depending on learning needs.

Information Problem

Any problem requiring information to solve. An information problem might be as simple as choosing which movie to go to on Saturday night, or as complex as discovering the causes of pollution in a community. Both problems require the accessing, evaluating, analyzing and synthesizing of information.

Information Literacy

Strategies and life skills that apply to the process of understanding, collecting, synthesizing and presenting information. It is an essential component of the teaching program in the library media center and is best taught in the context of the classroom curriculum in collaboration between the classroom teacher and the library media specialist.

Information Literacy Standards for Student Learning

Competencies that all students should achieve by the end of the 12th grade in order to be effective seekers and users of information. These national standards, defined by AASL and AECT, are part of *Information Power: Building Partners for Learning.* (See Information Literacy)

Inquiry

The process of formulating appropriate research questions, organizing the search for data, analyzing and evaluating the data found, and communicating the results in a coherent presentation.

Intellectual Freedom

Intellectual freedom is a prerequisite to effective and responsible citizenship in a democracy. Library media programs are committed to the right of intellectual freedom for all learners including an atmosphere of free inquiry and free access to information and ideas representing diverse points of view.

Interlibrary Loan

The process of locating and sharing resources beyond the school collection. This might involve obtaining resources for student and staff use from another school in the district, a public library, a state resource center, or a local university.

Internet Acceptable Use Policy

A policy adopted by the local board of education defining acceptable Internet activities and establishing students' rights and responsibilities on the Internet. This policy must be signed by a student's parents or guardian in order to grant student access to the Internet at school.

Library Media Program (LMP)

All the functions, resources, and responsibilities of the school library media center.

Library Media Specialist (LMS)

A professional staff person who holds a degree with a specialty in school library media and is licensed by the appropriate state agency.

Online Catalog

An electronic catalog and circulation system that replaces the traditional card catalog for the location of resources. It is often referred to as an OPAC or online public access catalog.

Selection Policy

A comprehensive district policy that provides the philosophy and general guidelines for the selection of all resources. The policy is the basis for collection development and challenged materials are reviewed in light of the district's selection policy. (See Collection Development)

Weeding

The process of culling resources from the library media program collection which are no longer relevant to the interests and learning needs of the school's students, teachers, staff, and community.

Policies That Determine the Quality of the Library Media Center Programs

Information Power: Building Partnerships for Learning contains several national policies including the ALA Library Bill of Rights, ALA Access to Resources and Services in the School Library Media Program, ALA Confidentiality of Library Records, the ALA Freedom to Read, AECT (Association for Educational Communications and Technology) Code of Ethics, and the AECT Statement on Intellectual Freedom.

During the development of the assessment rubric, it became apparent that district policies are in place that may be undefined and not in print. Nevertheless they serve as powerful determinants of the quality of programs. District policies provide the ground rules in determining whether a library media program falls into the Basic, Proficient, or Exemplary level. For example, the decision to allocate $20 pr student for library media resources instead of $5 per student results in a diverse, in-depth collection of resources. Students can then find materials needed to support their learning. Consideration should be given to each item listed here and district policy reexamined and redefined as appropriate.

- Collaboration opportunities among staff
- Participants in curriculum writing teams
- Inquiry based learning
- Student assessment process
- Student use of the library media center - Scheduling considerations
- Access to resources - Technology allocations
- Library media center facility design
- Library media program budget allocation
- Intellectual freedom policy
- Selection policy
- Collection development policy
- Internet use policy
- Professional and support staffing
- Administrative support
- Interlibrary loan
- Assessment of the library media program
- Volunteer policy
- Local and national staff development and training
- Opportunities for district meetings of library media specialists
- Participation in local library and education consortia

Bibliography

Planning and Implementation Resources

American Association of School Librarians. *Information Power: Because Student Learning is the Bottom Line*. Chicago: American Association of School Librarians, 1998. 66p. $10.00.
A national plan for coordinating the implementation of *Information Power: Building Partnerships for Learning*. A model that can be adapted to district and building level implementation plans.

American Association of School Librarians and Association for Educational Communications and Technology. *Information Power: Building Partnerships for Learning*. Chicago: American Library Association, 1998. 224p. $35.00.
National guidelines and principles that will help create a dynamic, student-centered school library media program that will help students become skillful producers and consumers of information. Divided into two parts, part one of the publication is "*Information Literacy Standards for Student Learning*," which is also published separately. Part two is "Building Partnerships for Learning."

American Association of School Librarians and Association for Educational Communications and Technology. *Information Literacy Standards for Student Learning*. Chicago: American Library Association, 1998. 64p. $20.00.
Contains the vision and mission statements for school library media programs, the four roles of the library media specialist, and the *Information Literacy Standards for Student Learning* which consist of three categories, nine standards, and twenty-nine indicators.

Bradburn, Frances Bryant. *Output Measures for School Library Media Programs*. New York: Neal Schuman, 1999. 95p. $49.95.
Output Measures contains a variety of procedures that can analyze and document what works and what does not work within the library media program. The first section defines and explains the data collection methods. The second contains case studies that simulate the data-gathering and presentation process.

Fitzpatrick, Kathleen A. *Program Evaluation: Library Media Services*. Schaumburg, Ill.: National Study of School Evaluation, 1998. 130p. $30.00.
Developed by NSSE in collaboration with the Alliance for Curriculum Reform and representatives of the American Association of School Librarians, this volume of the *Program Evaluation Series* provides guidelines, focus questions, worksheets, and checklists which can guide the evaluation of library media services.

Johnson, Doug. *The Indispensable Librarian: Surviving (And Thriving) in School Media Centers*. Worthington, Ohio: Linworth Publishing Co., 1997. 163p. $36.95.
This workbook provides outlines, checklists, and samples and covers planning, public relations, mission, budget, and policies. Provides space for your own notes.

Stripling, Barbara, ed. *Learning and Libraries in an Information Age: Principles and Practice*. Englewood, Colo.: Libraries Unlimited, 1999.
To be published November 1999.

Valenza, Joyce Kasman. *Power Tools 100+ Essential Forms and Presentations for Your School Library Information*. Chicago: American Library Association, 1998. 272p. $45.00.
Provides templates of forms for everything from library passes to rubrics for research papers. The package contains a booklet and CD-ROM that cover public relations, day-to-day operations, information skills, graphic organizers, and the Internet.

Wasman, Anne. *New Steps to Service: Common-Sense Advice for the School Library Media Specialist*. Chicago: American Library Association, 1998. 256p. $20.00.
Although intended for new library media specialists, this is a comprehensive resource about running a school library media center. It covers such topics as acquisitions, cataloging, budgeting, and public relations.

Yesner, Bernice and Hilda L. Jay. *Operating and Evaluating School Library Media Programs: A Handbook for Administrators and Librarians*. New York: Neal Schuman, 1998. 424p. $49.95.
Administrators, school library media specialists, and teachers can use this book as a tool to assess the effectiveness of the school library media program. Each topic contains a brief statement of current practices with a checklist providing a self-evaluation tool for school library media specialists. The book also contains sample evaluation forms.